D0754641

T3-AZM-748

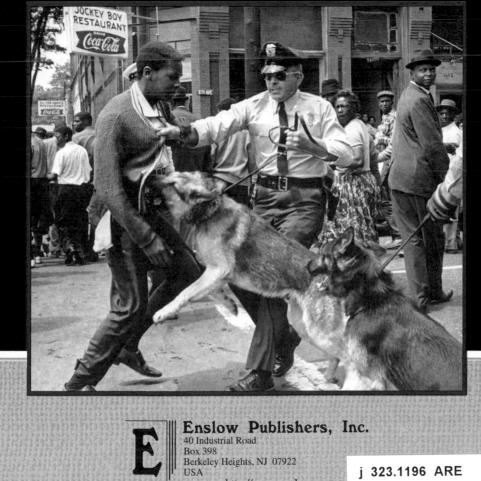

Library of Congress Cataloging-in-Publication Data

Aretha, David.
  The story of the Birmingham civil rights movement in photographs / David Aretha.
    pages cm. — (The story of the civil rights movement in photographs)
  Includes index.
  Summary: "Examines the Birmingham Civil Rights Movement, including the organizers of the protests, the movement's support from young people, the violence that occurred, and the integration of Birmingham"—Provided by publisher.
  ISBN 978-0-7660-4237-7
  1. African Americans—Civil rights—Alabama—Birmingham—History—20th century—Pictorial works—Juvenile literature. 2. African American civil rights workers—Alabama—Birmingham—Biography—Pictorial works—Juvenile literature. 3. Civil rights movements—Alabama—Birmingham—History—20th century—Pictorial works—Juvenile literature. 4. Birmingham (Ala.)—Race relations—Pictorial works—Juvenile literature. I. Title.
  F334.B69N414 2014
  323.1196'0730761781—dc23
                            2012050435

Future editions:
Paperback ISBN: 978-1-4644-0417-7   Single-User PDF ISBN: 978-1-4646-1228-2
EPUB ISBN: 978-1-4645-1228-5   Multi-User PDF ISBN: 978-0-7660-5860-6

Printed in the United States of America

112013 Bang Printing, Brainerd, Minn.

10 9 8 7 6 5 4 3 2 1

To Our Readers: We have done our best to make sure all Internet Addresses in this book were active and appropriate when we went to press. However, the author and the publisher have no control over and assume no liability for the material available on those Internet sites or on other Web sites they may link to. Any comments or suggestions can be sent by e-mail to comments@enslow.com or to the address on the back cover.

♻ Enslow Publishers, Inc., is committed to printing our books on recycled paper. The paper in every book contains 10% to 30% post-consumer waste (PCW). The cover board on the outside of each book contains 100% PCW. Our goal is to do our part to help young people and the environment too!

Illustration Credits: AP Images, pp. 8, 18, 26, 33, 34 (top and bottom), 38–39, 40 (top and bottom); AP Images / Bill Hudson, pp. 1, 20–21, 22, 24–25, 28–29, 30, 46 (middle), 47; AP Images / Charles Gorry, p. 36; AP Images / Corbis Bettman, p. 23; AP Images / Horace Cort, pp. 3, 4, 12, 13, 14–15; AP Images / PFO, pp. 2, 10, 11; AP Images / Richard Dew, p. 16; National Archives and Records Administration, pp. 16 (inset), 42, 46 (top and bottom).

Cover Illustration: AP Images / Bill Hudson (May 3, 1963, police dogs attack Walter Gadsden, a seventeen-year-old civil rights activist, during a demonstration in Birmingham, Alabama).

Table of Contents

African Americans chant "Freedom" in Albany, Georgia, on July 25, 1962. Many would participate in a segregation protest the following day.

Introduction

By 1963, Birmingham, Alabama, had earned the nickname "Bombingham." The reason? White racists in that city had a history of bombing the homes and churches of African Americans. Civil rights leaders were determined to end the oppression of black citizens. In 1963, they focused on Birmingham.

Slavery had ended in 1865. But in the South, segregation remained over the next hundred years. A segregated society means that the dominant racial group separates and mistreats a less-powerful group. In southern states, whites held all the positions of high-level leadership. They made rules that benefited their race. They segregated the schools, restaurants, libraries, drinking fountains, parks, pools, and more. In the segregated South, facilities for black citizens were not only separate, they were inferior.

Thanks to the great efforts of civil rights activists, some facilities in the South had become desegregated by 1963. For example, many whites-only lunch counters in stores were now open to black customers. But not in Birmingham. Reverend Martin Luther King, Jr., called Alabama's largest city the most segregated city in America.

Birmingham had a population of 350,000, 40 percent of whom were African American. Besides segregated facilities, black people faced other injustices and humiliations in Birmingham. Whites hired African Americans only for manual-labor jobs, housecleaning, and other low-paying positions. The average income of black workers was less than half that of whites.

Whites in Alabama and other southern states devised ways to keep black people from voting. For example, they threatened to fire them from their jobs if they tried to cast ballots. In 1960, only 10 percent of Birmingham's black population was registered to vote.

All of Birmingham's police officers were white. If black citizens "got out of line," they could be beaten by police officers or members of the Ku Klux Klan—an all-white hate group. African-American reverend Fred Shuttlesworth tried to fight the injustice, forming the Alabama Christian Movement for Human Rights (ACMHR) in 1956. That December, Shuttlesworth organized a protest of Birmingham's segregated buses. Segregationists responded by bombing his house, nearly killing him. On other occasions, they beat him with chains and brass knuckles, and they stabbed his wife.

Shuttlesworth wrote about the violence that African Americans faced: "We have always been a peaceful people, bearing our oppression with super-human effort. Yet we have been the victims of repeated violence, not only that inflicted by the hoodlum element but also that inflicted by the blatant misuse of police power. . . . For years, while our homes and churches were being bombed, we heard nothing but the rantings and ravings of racist city officials."

Martin Luther King, Jr., hoped to end the injustice. Having led the successful fight against racial segregation in the bus system of Montgomery, Alabama (1955–1956), King, by 1963, was the most prominent civil rights leader in America. A charismatic speaker, he urged African Americans to fight against racial injustice—but to do so through nonviolent means. King led a civil rights organization called the Southern Christian Leadership Conference (SCLC).

In 1961 and 1962, King and the SCLC organized a series of protest marches in segregated Albany, Georgia. They hoped it would capture the nation's attention and inspire Americans to demand an end to segregation. However, the Albany campaign did not generate national interest. Police arrested protesters, but they treated them humanely. Americans were not outraged, like King had hoped.

In early 1963, King believed that a campaign in Birmingham would produce different results. He predicted that Americans would be outraged because police would abuse civil rights protesters. In May 1961, Birmingham Public Safety Commissioner Eugene "Bull" Connor had allowed a white mob to beat civil rights activists with metal pipes. If law officers or Ku Klux Klansmen attacked peaceful protesters, photographers and film crews would record the violence. The nation's citizens would be shocked, King predicted. Americans would urge the federal (U.S.) government to end racial injustice in the South.

The courageous Shuttlesworth worked with King and the SCLC. They called the upcoming civil rights campaign Project C—for Confrontation. Shuttlesworth issued the "Birmingham Manifesto." It stated in part: "We appeal to the citizenry of Birmingham, Negro and white, to join us in this witness for decency, morality, self-respect and human dignity. Your individual and corporate support can hasten the day of 'liberty and justice for all.'"

Project C would begin on April 3, 1963. The confrontations would soon follow, and Americans would indeed be appalled.

Chapter 1

The Battles
BEGIN

Black and white citizens stroll through downtown Birmingham in the spring of 1963.

Committed to Segregation

The people of Birmingham were hard workers. The local mills produced tons of iron and steel—more than any area in the South. Unfortunately for African Americans, segregation in Birmingham was as strong as iron. Black citizens lived in the worst parts of the city. Local government devoted less money to the upkeep of black neighborhoods. After a federal court ordered that dozens of city parks admit black citizens, city officials responded by closing those parks. They did the same for public playgrounds, swimming pools, and golf courses.

The Ku Klux Klan, a racist hate group, was active in Birmingham. Since World War II, KKK members had bombed dozens of buildings, including many African-American churches. One black neighborhood was bombed so often it was called "Dynamite Hill." In 1956, legendary African-American singer Nat King Cole was beaten on stage by segregationists. For the SCLC, trying to change Birmingham would be a violent struggle.

Reverend Fred Shuttlesworth was frequently arrested for protesting segregation. "I was in jail so many times," he said, "I quit counting after twenty."

Shuttlesworth Leads the Way

Reverend Fred Shuttlesworth and the ACMHR had fought successfully against segregation in Birmingham. "We had desegregated the buses and terminals, and done many other things," he said in *Voices of Freedom*. He felt that with the SCLC's help, African Americans could make more gains in his city—and elsewhere. "Birmingham is where it's at, gentlemen," he told the SCLC.

The "Birmingham Manifesto"

The SCLC launched Project C in early April. Their "Birmingham Manifesto" included their goals. They demanded that all businesses in the city be desegregated. They also wanted the city to adopt fair-hiring practices. African Americans, they insisted, should not be denied jobs based on their skin color. On April 3, black activists staged sit-ins at local stores.

On April 4, 1963, college student Dorothy Bell, waits for service at a whites-only lunch counter in Birmingham. Bell and twenty others were arrested.

Marching to City Hall

Tensions increased in Birmingham on April 6. That day, forty-five protesters were arrested as they marched to city hall. The next day, police arrested more demonstrators. Local leaders didn't want these protests to go any further. That week, Judge W. A. Jenkins issued an order preventing 133 of the city's civil rights leaders from organizing more demonstrations. Martin Luther King, Jr., was on the list.

Connor Shows No Mercy

Bull Connor recently lost his bid to become mayor of Birmingham. However, he remained the city's public safety commissioner. In that role, he was in charge of the police and fire departments. A hard-line segregationist, Connor showed no mercy to the civil rights activists. He ordered police to arrest marchers, even if they were protesting peacefully. Connor had once declared that segregation "will be enforced in Birmingham to the utmost of my ability. . . ."

Public Safety Commissioner Bull Connor directs the arrest of approximately twenty-five African-American demonstrators on April 10.

1 B

In that dramatic scene on Calvary's hill three men were crucified. We must never forget that all three were crucified for the same crime — the crime of extremism. Two were extremists for immorality, and thus fell below their environment. The other, Jesus Christ, was an extremist for love, truth, and goodness, and thereby rose above his environment.

2 B

I have been so greatly disappointed with the white church and its leadership. Of course there are some notable exceptions. I am not unmindful of the fact that each of you has taken some significant stand

"Letter From a Birmingham Jail"

Martin Luther King, Jr., loved to write. He had plenty of time to do so while in solitary confinement in a Birmingham jail. Writing on newspaper margins and scraps of paper, King penned "Letter From a Birmingham Jail." It was a response to white clergymen who had said that the Birmingham demonstrations were "unwise and untimely."

King said that "after more than 340 years," black Americans could no longer just wait and hope for equal rights. He wrote:

> . . . when you suddenly find your tongue twisted and your speech stammering as you seek to explain to your six-year-old daughter why she can't go to the public amusement park that has just been advertised on television, and see tears welling up in her eyes when she is told that Funtown is closed to colored children . . . , when you have to concoct an answer for a five-year-old son who is asking: "Daddy, why do white people treat colored people so mean?" . . . then you will understand why we find it difficult to wait.

"Letter From a Birmingham Jail" was first published in a New York magazine on May 19, 1963. Millions of people would be moved by his emotional words.

Martin Luther King, Jr., penned this letter while locked in a Birmingham jail.

The Birmingham campaign was losing steam until preacher James Bevel (pictured) came up with an idea. Students, he said, should march in Birmingham. Children volunteered by the hundreds.

Send the Children

On April 20, King and fellow SCLC leader Ralph Abernathy were released from jail. They found that the movement had stalled while they had been behind bars. Only a few people a day had been demonstrating. James Bevel, a fiery preacher and SCLC organizer, understood the problem. Most adults in Birmingham, he said, didn't want to march because they could be arrested. And in Birmingham, employers were known to fire workers who were civil rights activists.

According to Bevel in *Voices of Freedom*, "the strategy was, Okay, let's use *thousands* of people who won't create an economic crisis because they're off the job: *the high school students*." It would be dubbed the "Children's Crusade." Birmingham's students would march downtown. The plan was controversial. As Malcolm X, a famous civil rights leader, said: "Real men don't put their children on the firing line."

However, Birmingham's black students volunteered in large numbers. According to Bevel, the high school girls were the first to respond, followed by elementary school students. The last to get involved were the high school boys, because police were more likely to abuse them.

Bevel said that they held workshops to help students "overcome the crippling fears of dogs, and jails, and to help them start thinking through problems on their feet." The marches would begin on May 2.

Chapter 3

The Children's CRUSADE

Busing Kids to Jail

On May 2, children ages six to eighteen gathered at the Sixteenth Street Baptist Church. Martin Luther King, Jr., talked to the children, saying he was proud of them. Soon, the kids began marching while singing "freedom songs." Under Bull Connor's orders, police arrested the marchers and sent them to jail. Yet more children kept on marching.

Police arrested these students after a "Children's Crusade" march in early May. Police arrested so many children on May 2 that they ran out of paddy wagons. They had to use school buses to take away all the young "lawbreakers." On May 2, by the end of the day, 959 young people had been arrested.

Birmingham's fire chief did not want to turn hoses on the children. But, according to the book *Carry Me Home*, Connor told the chief: "Turn 'em on, or go home."

Blasted With Hoses

On May 3, more than a thousand students gathered for another march. This time, Connor wanted to stop the demonstration before it began, using police dogs and fire hoses. Firefighters blasted children with the water, injuring some of them. The streams were so powerful that one boy's shirt was ripped right off. Others were pinned against buildings, knocked over cars, or rolled down the street.

Two young protesters try to avoid the blast of a fire hose. The water was strong enough to break a person's ribs.

On May 4, 1963, the *New York Times* published this photo on its front page. It shows police dogs attacking a high school student named Walter Gadsden. Bull Connor had ordered police to bring out the dogs, hoping they would scare students so much that they wouldn't march. They marched anyway. Police dogs tore the clothes and flesh of the demonstrators. One protester attempted to fight off one of the dogs with a knife, but police knocked the young man down and kicked him.

After the jails were full, police sent students to outdoor jail yards despite cool, damp weather. Condoleezza Rice, the future U.S. Secretary of State, lived in Birmingham. As an eight-year-old, she saw these children "huddled beneath tents."

Chapter 4

Descending Into CHAOS

Soaked and Screaming

The scene in downtown Birmingham on May 3 was pure chaos. Young protesters, soaked with water, were screaming. Police dogs attacked others. More than a thousand black onlookers booed the officers. From a rooftop, some African Americans rained bricks and bottles down on police. A white man tried to drive his car into a gathering of marchers. Police officers barricaded a thousand black citizens in a church, preventing them from marching. Finally, at around 3 P.M., tensions eased. James Bevel, through a police bullhorn, urged black citizens to get off the streets. Eventually, they did.

These girls were arrested and sent to this building at the county fairgrounds. Many students *wanted* to be arrested. To them, it was the ultimate way of protesting against segregation.

Arrests Increase and Spirits Soar

On Saturday, May 4, photos from Birmingham made the front pages of newspapers all over the country. Americans were astonished to view pictures of young people abused by police and firefighters. "I can see," President John F. Kennedy said, "why the Negroes of Birmingham are tired of being patient."

The battles in Birmingham were far from over. Parents of jailed children seethed in anger. At a demonstration on May 4, some brought guns and knives. James Bevel had to calm them down. "Okay, get off the streets now," he said through a bullhorn. "We're not going to have violence." However, marches did continue, and so did the arrests. Through May 6, more than two thousand protesters had been jailed.

On the evening of May 6, Martin Luther King, Jr., spoke at a packed church. He praised the citizens for their courageous actions. "Never in the history of this nation," he declared, "have so many people been arrested for the cause of freedom and human dignity!" The church erupted in applause.

Protests and arrests occurred every day from May 2 to May 7. On May 7, these young women sing, "I want to be free."

An Agreement Is Reached

On May 7, demonstrations continued on Birmingham's streets. "I was afraid of getting hurt, but still I was willing to march on to have justice done," said student Patricia Harris in *Voices of Freedom*. Once again, firefighters turned hoses on the protesters. Reverend Fred Shuttlesworth was injured so badly by a water blast that he had to go to the hospital. According to *Eyes on the Prize*, Connor smiled when he heard about Shuttlesworth's injury. "I'm sorry I missed it," Connor said.

TV cameras recorded the drama in Birmingham. Images of attack dogs and fire hoses were shown on the TV news. Viewers felt that these attacks were wrong. Many Americans were realizing that segregation in the South had to end—and soon.

President Kennedy sent Burke Marshall to Birmingham to reach a peaceful settlement. Marshall was head of the U.S. Justice Department's Civil Rights Division. Marshall negotiated with the Senior Citizens Committee, a group that represented most of Birmingham's businesses. Concerned about damage to their downtown stores, committee members agreed to the demands of the SCLC. They would desegregate local stores and hire black workers. In return, civil rights leaders ended the demonstrations. King called the agreement "the most significant victory for justice that we have seen in the Deep South."

Unfortunately, this wasn't the end of the story in Birmingham. Not by a long shot.

Chapter 5

Violent REACTIONS

Connor Rejects the Settlement

On May 10, Martin Luther King, Jr., and Fred Shuttlesworth held a news conference in Birmingham. They announced the agreement that had been reached with the Senior Citizens Committee. Within ninety days, the city's lunch counters, fitting rooms, restrooms, and drinking fountains would be desegregated. All jailed protesters would be released. And businesses would begin to hire black workers in downtown stores. Bull Connor, however, thought that the committee members were traitors. He asked Birmingham's white citizens not to shop at downtown stores. Alabama governor George Wallace also opposed the settlement.

Martin Luther King, Jr., tells reporters about the Birmingham agreement. Segregationists fumed with anger over the decision.

President John F. Kennedy addresses the nation on television on June 11, 1963. Kennedy said he would urge Congress to pass a strong civil rights bill. It was time, he said, to end segregation.

Support From the Court

On May 20, 1963, civil rights lawyers scored a major victory. The U.S. Supreme Court ruled that segregation laws in American cities were unconstitutional. That meant they were against U.S. law. But it didn't mean that Southerners would follow that law. The Supreme Court had outlawed segregated schooling in 1954, but southern school systems were still almost entirely segregated in 1963.

Alabama governor George Wallace resisted integration. "Segregation forever!" he once declared. On June 11, 1963, Wallace stood in front of a doorway at the University of Alabama. In a symbolic gesture, he prevented Vivian Malone and James Hood from becoming the first African Americans to attend the school.

That night, President Kennedy addressed the nation on television. He wanted to announce his support for equal rights for African Americans. He said that he would ask Congress to create laws "giving all Americans the right to be served in facilities which are open to the public—hotels, restaurants, theaters, retail stores, and similar establishments."

Martin Luther King, Jr., knew that southern Congress members would strongly resist a civil rights bill. He wanted to show Congress that the American people supported such a bill. The best way to do that, he believed, was for thousands of Americans to "march" to Washington.

Chapter 6

A Triumph in
WASHINGTON

King: "I Have a Dream"

The outrage surrounding the Birmingham campaign contributed to the March on Washington for Jobs and Freedom. On August 28, 1963, some 250,000 people, black and white, demonstrated in the nation's capital. They sang "freedom songs," such as "We Shall Overcome" and "Ain't Gon' Let Nobody Turn Me Around." Martin Luther King, Jr., during his famous "I Have a Dream" speech, might still have been thinking of Birmingham when he said: "I have a dream that one day, down in Alabama, with its vicious racists . . . little black boys and black girls will be able to join hands with little white boys and white girls as sisters and brothers."

The March on Washington attracted freedom lovers from all over the nation. Their demands for justice helped inspire Congress members to pass an anti-segregation bill.

Alabama Resists Integration

On the morning of September 15, 1963, a bomb exploded at the Sixteenth Street Baptist Church in Birmingham. Four African-American girls were killed and twenty other people were wounded. Robert "Dynamite Bob" Chambliss of the Ku Klux Klan was among a group of men who planted the bomb. (They would not be convicted of the crime until many years later.)

These men, and most whites in Alabama, still resisted desegregation. This was especially true when it came to schools. Earlier in 1963, a federal court had ordered several public school systems in Alabama to accept African-American students. On September 4, two black students enrolled at Birmingham's Graymont Elementary School. Many white parents were so upset that they took their students out of Graymont. Nearby that day, the house of a black lawyer was bombed.

By the mid-1960s, southern whites largely accepted integrated buses, stores, and restaurants. But they resisted integrated schools for much longer. Many white parents did not want their children learning with, befriending, or dating black students. By 1964, only one percent of Alabama's black students were attending school with whites.

TOP LEFT: Chris and Maxine McNair hold a picture of their daughter, Denise. She was killed in the church bombing.

BOTTOM LEFT: Denise McNair was eleven years old. The other three girls who died in the bombing were fourteen. They were (left to right) Carole Robertson, Addie Mae Collins, and Cynthia Wesley.

President Lyndon B. Johnson signs the 1964 Civil Rights Act. He would give one of the "signing pens" on his desk to Martin Luther King, Jr., who stands behind him.

Victory at Last

By the end of 1963, many civil rights activists were losing hope. President Kennedy's proposed civil rights bill had not been passed. Though Birmingham had integrated its stores, many southern cities and towns still had not. Southern schools remained almost entirely segregated. Then, on November 22, 1963, President Kennedy was assassinated.

No president in history had supported civil rights as strongly as Kennedy had. Black Americans had lost a "friend" in the White House. However, new president Lyndon Johnson was determined to promote the passage of strong civil rights laws. He stated that "no memorial, oration, or eulogy could more eloquently honor President Kennedy's memory than the earliest possible passage of the civil rights bill for which he fought so long."

On July 2, 1964, President Johnson signed the civil rights bill into law. This Civil Rights Act banned segregation in public places throughout the United States. It also gave the U.S. government more power to enforce anti-segregation laws. "My fellow citizens," Johnson declared, "we have come to a time of testing. We must not fail. Let us close the springs of racial poison."

African Americans rejoiced. After years of marches and sit-ins—after being beaten and sent to jail—civil rights activists were getting close to achieving their ultimate dream: true freedom.

Conclusion

In 1963, a young white woman from New York named Gloria Clark watched the events unfold in Birmingham. She remembered watching Bull Connor being interviewed on television. She said: "I've never forgotten this line: 'We can take care of our nigras ourselves.' . . . And I said no way is he going to define how people are treated in the country I live in. No way do I want a man like that defining it."

Like Gloria Clark, millions of Americans were upset by the injustice in Birmingham. As mentioned, 250,000 Americans marched to Washington in August 1963. The following year, Clark and hundreds of other black and white activists staged "Freedom Summer" in Mississippi. They worked to get African Americans registered to vote. They strived to give black children a proper education in what they called "Freedom Schools." Segregationists killed four Freedom Summer volunteers in 1964, but the activists did not back down.

In 1965, the SCLC led a movement in Selma, Alabama, that was similar to the Birmingham campaign. This time, it was about voting rights. Civil rights activists demanded an end to voting discrimination in that city. As in Birmingham, the Selma police arrested hundreds of civil rights activists. Others were assaulted with clubs, tear gas, and cattle prods. Two people were killed.

Still, the activists—black and white—persevered. They planned to march fifty-four miles from Selma to Montgomery, Alabama. "March together, children," Martin Luther King, Jr., declared on March 21. "Don't you get weary, and it will lead us to the Promised Land. And Alabama will be a new Alabama, and America will be a new America!"

Their courageous walk for justice inspired more Americans to call for an end to segregation. In 1965, Congress passed the Voting Rights Act. With the new law in place, segregationists could no longer prevent African Americans from voting. The Civil Rights Act of 1964, coupled with the Voting Rights Act of 1965, largely ended segregation in the South. "Colored" and "Whites Only" signs came down. Black citizens could eat at any restaurant, sit where they pleased on buses, and vote in elections.

However, true equality was still hard to come by. African Americans in Birmingham, and throughout the South, still had huge obstacles to overcome. Most worked for low wages—if they could find a job at all. Few had a college education or could afford to go to college. Even though segregation was behind them, most black families found it difficult to pull themselves out of poverty.

Gradually, many families did. In the United States, the high school graduation rate for African Americans rose from 20 percent in 1960 to 50 percent in 1980. With segregation a thing of the past, black citizens finally were hired as police officers, government workers, and many other previously closed jobs.

Today, African Americans in the South thrive in all professions—from business to medicine to law. However, the average black citizen in Birmingham and the United States still makes less money than the average white American. A large problem is that it is still hard to escape poverty. Schools and learning environments in poor neighborhoods are not what they should be. While the high school graduation rate for whites is about 82 percent, it is only about 63 percent for black students.

Sharrif Simmons, a teacher in Birmingham, sees that problem in his city. "Obviously, the racism today is not as blatant as it was in the past," he said. "Where I see it manifested most clearly is in the school system. . . . In the suburbs, the white students are equipped with all the latest technology, new facilities, and uncrowded classrooms. In the inner city, the black students experience the opposite conditions."

In Birmingham and throughout the U.S., the story is the same: African Americans have achieved equal rights, but they are still seeking true equality.

Civil Rights Movement Timeline

1865–1965: After slavery, African Americans in the South are confined to segregated (separate, inferior) facilities. They are denied citizenship rights, such as voting.

1954: The U.S. Supreme Court bans segregation in public schools.

1955–1956: Martin Luther King, Jr., leads a successful yearlong boycott of segregated buses in Montgomery, Alabama.

1957: The National Guard helps black students integrate Central High School in Little Rock, Arkansas.

1960–mid-1960s: Civil rights activists stage hundreds of sit-ins at segregated restaurants, stores, theaters, libraries, and many other establishments.

1961: Activists stage Freedom Rides on segregated buses in the South.

1963: Thousands of African Americans protest segregation in Birmingham, Alabama.

1963: A quarter-million Americans attend the March on Washington for Jobs and Freedom in Washington, D.C.

1964: Activists register black voters in Mississippi during "Freedom Summer."

1964: The U.S. Congress passes the Civil Rights Act. It outlaws segregation and other racial injustices.

1965: African Americans protest voting injustice in Selma, Alabama.

1965: Congress passes the Voting Rights Act, which guarantees voting rights for all Americans.

Further Reading

Books

Brimner, Larry Dane. *Black and White: The Confrontation Between Reverend Fred L. Shuttlesworth and Eugene "Bull" Connor.* Honesdale, Pa.: Boyds Mill Press, 2011.

Levinson, Cynthia. *We've Got a Job: The 1963 Birmingham Children's March.* Atlanta: Peachtree Publishers, 2012.

Levine, Ellen H. *Freedom's Children: Young Civil Rights Activists Tell Their Own Stories.* New York, NY: Penguin Youn Readers, 2000.

Tougas, Shelley. *Birmingham 1963: How a Photograph Rallied Civil Rights Support.* Mankato, Minn.: Compass Point Books, 2011.

Internet Addresses

Birmingham Civil Rights Institute
<http://www.bcri.org/index.html>

The Martin Luther King, Jr., Center for Nonviolent Social Change
<http://www.thekingcenter.org/>

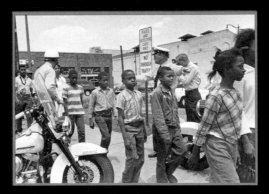

Index